CONTE.

GU00818482

SOUPS

Cauliflower	P.2
Onion & mushroom	P.2
Gazpacho	P.3
Curried parsnip	P.3

FISH

Haddock soup	P.4
Fish cakes	P.5
Fish pie with apple	P.5
Mackerel quiche	P.6

MAIN DISHES

Mushroom flan	P.7
Quinoa risotto	P.8
Pepper & tofu salad	P.9
Pasta & tomato sauce	P.9
Pasta Primavera	P.10
Spinach soufflé	P.11
Chicken apple salad	P.11
Chicken crumble/pie	P.12
Chicken with okra	P.13
Barbecues	P.13
Stir fries	P.14
Egg free moussaka	P.15
Braised lamb	P.16
Potato & polenta bake	P.17
Hints with vegetables	P.17

XMAS DISHES

Quinoa stuffing	P.19
Gravy	P.19
Chickpea stuffing	P.20
Miriam's mince tart	P.21

Xmas

Gluten-free Xmas pud.	P.22
Brandy butter	P.22
Miriam's fruit cake	P.23

DESSERTS

Dairy free rice pud.	P.24
Suedoise of peaches	P.25
Apple soufflé	P.26
Gluten free apple flan	P.26
Tofu cheesecake	P.27
Soya milk shake	P.27
Soya fruit fool	P.28
Red fruit salad	P.28
Fruit & nut crumble	P.29
Hot fruit compote	P.29
Dairy free profiteroles	P.30
Gooey choccy mousse	P.31
Carob 'chocolates'	P.31

BAKING

Eggless fruit cake	P.32
Oat flapjacks	P.33
Lemon shortbread	P.34
Lemon or orange cake	P.34
Chocolate cake	P.35
Oat gingerbread	P.35
Oat-based pastry	P.36
Oat bread	P.36
Gluten-free loaf	P.37
Rice 'bread sauce'	P.18
Gluten-free pastry	P.37

PRODUCT DIRECTORY

P.37 - 41

SOUPS

CAULIFLOWER AND HORSERADISH SOUP
Serves 4 - generously
Dairy free; gluten free; egg free; low fat; 19 Kcal/portion
1 medium onion, chopped
350g/12 oz cauliflower, florets and stalk
1 litre/35fl oz water
2 heaped tbsp horseradish sauce (check ingredients list for gluten)
salt and pepper
4 tbsp chopped parsley (optional)
1. Put the onion and cauliflower in a pan with the water, bring it to the boil and simmer it for 30 minutes. Purée it in a processor, liquidiser or mouli legumes and return it to the pan.
2. Mix the horseradish in a small bowl with a little of the soup till you get a smooth paste then add it to the soup along with seasoning to taste - you will need quite a lot.
3. Serve it as it is or add the chopped parsley just before you serve it.

CLEAR ONION AND MUSHROOM SOUP
Serves 6
Dairy free; gluten free; egg free; low fat; 137 Kcal/portion
3 tbsp olive or other good vegetable oil
350g/12oz onions, finely sliced
350g/12oz open mushrooms, chopped small
450ml/15 fl oz dry white wine
1.2 litres/40fl oz water
salt and pepper
1. Melt the oil in a heavy pan, add the onions and mushrooms and cook very slowly till they are both quite soft.
2. Add the wine and water, bring to the boil, season lightly and simmer for 30 - 35 minutes.
3. Adjust seasoning to taste and serve.

GAZPACHO

Serves 6
Dairy free; gluten free; egg free; low fat; 199 Kcal/portion
1 kilo/2lb ripe tomatoes, chopped roughly
3 large cloves garlic
1 small onion, finely chopped
6 tbsp olive oil
300ml/10fl oz dry white wine
600ml/1pt chicken or vegetable stock
juice 1 - 2 lemons
salt and pepper
25-50g/1-2oz each finely chopped celery, red pepper and cucumber

1. Put the tomatoes in a large pan with the garlic, onion, oil, wine and stock. Bring to the boil and simmer for 1 hour.
2. Purée the soup in a food processor or liquidiser then put through a sieve to remove the pips.
3. Add lemon juice, salt and pepper to taste bearing in mind that flavours get dulled by chilling.
4. Chill the soup and just before serving add the chopped vegetables.

CURRIED PARSNIP AND APPLE SOUP

Serves 6
Dairy free; gluten free; egg free; low fat; 154 Kcal/portion
3 tbsp vegetable oil
1 tbsp gluten free curry powder
225g/8oz leeks, sliced
450g/1lb parsnips, scrubbed and sliced thinly
225g/8oz cooking apple, peeled and chopped
1.5 litres/2 1/2 pts chicken or vegetable stock
150ml/5fl oz each milk/soya milk and dry white wine
salt and pepper
2 tart eating apples

1. Heat oil in a heavy bottomed pan, stir in the curry powder, then the leeks and parsnips and cooking apple.
2. Cook all together gently without burning for 10 - 15 minutes or till the leeks are quite soft and the parsnips softening.
3. Add the stock, milk and wine, bring to the boil and simmer for 30 - 35 minutes or till the parsnips are quite cooked then purée in a processor.
5. Reheat and adjust the seasoning to taste. Just before serving add the two eating apples, peeled and chopped finely.

FISH

FENNEL AND HADDOCK SOUP
Serves 6 - 8
Dairy free; gluten free; egg free; low fat; 171 Kcal/portion

3 tbsp olive or good vegetable oil
1 medium head of fennel, sliced very finely
4 large spring onions, sliced very finely
4 large anchovy fillets, chopped small
100g/4oz mushrooms, sliced
1.5litres/2 1/2 pints water
300ml/10fl oz dry white wine
225g/8oz fresh haddock fillets
100g/4oz tofu (optional)
juice 1/2 lemon
salt and freshly ground black pepper

1. Heat the oil in a large pan and gently cook the fennel, spring onions and anchovy fillets till they are soft but not coloured.
2. Add the mushrooms and continue to cook for a few minutes. Add the water and wine and bring slowly to the boil.
3. Meanwhile cut the fish into fairly large pieces.
4. When the soup has reached the boil add the fish and bring back to the boil; simmer for 5 minutes.
5. If you are using it, drain and chop the tofu into squares (2cm/1.2 inch squares would be quite big enough) and add it to the soup along with the lemon juice and seasoning.
6. Cook for minute or two then leave aside for a couple of hours for the flavours to mature.
7. Reheat to serve.

FISH CAKES

Makes 10 - 12 fish cakes
Dairy free; gluten free; egg free; medium fat; 153 Kcal / cake
450g/1lb white fish - cod, haddock, coley etc
100g/4oz brown rice
2 tbsp creme fraiche OR plain live yoghurt OR silken tofu
salt and pepper and the juice 1/2 lemon (optional)
Crumb coating: 3 tbsp polenta
*   1 pkt plain potato crisps, crushed*
3 - 4 tbsp olive, rape, sunflower or soya oil
1. Cook the rice in boiling water till it is very soft, then drain.
2. Purée the fish with the rice, creme fraiche, yoghurt or tofu, then season generously with salt, pepper and lemon juice. Chill thoroughly.
3. Mix the polenta with the crushed crisps in a flat dish.
4. Form generous dessertspoonfuls of the fish mixture into cakes and coat them with the polenta and crisp mix.
5. Fry the fish cakes gently in the oil for approximately 5 minutes on each side then serve at once accompanied by green vegetables or a green salad.

FISH PIE WITH APPLE

Serves 4
Dairy free; gluten free; egg free; low fat; 153 Kcal/portion
1kilo/2lbs potatoes, scrubbed
a little dairy free margarine
3 tbsp olive, soya, sunflower or rapeseed oil
2 large leeks, cleaned and thinly sliced
1 large cooking apple, peeled, cored and sliced thinly
4 fillets of sole, cod or other white fish
1 tbsp sunflower seeds
salt and pepper
1. Steam or boil the potatoes. Skin them, or not as you prefer, and mash them with a little margarine and seasoning.
2. Pour the oil into the bottom of an ovenproof pie or casserole dish and scatter the leeks over the bottom. Cover the leeks with the sliced apple and lay the fish fillets over the top. Season lightly.
4. Cover the fish with potato and sprinkle over the sunflower seeds. Dribble on a few drops of oil.
5. Bake in a moderate oven (180C/350F/Gas Mark 4) for 45 minutes or in a microwave on High for 15 minutes. If you cook it in a microwave the top will not brown.
6. Serve with a green vegetable or salad.

SMOKED MACKEREL AND TOFU 'QUICHE'

Serves 4

Dairy free; wheat free; egg free; high fat; 465 Kcal/portion

15-20cm/6-8 inch pastry case made from wheat, oat or gluten free paste
*   - see p.36/7 - baked blind*
1 tbsp olive oil
50g/2oz mushrooms, chopped roughly
300g/10oz silken tofu
180ml/6fl oz soya milk or 90ml/3fl oz each soya milk & dry white wine
1 smoked mackerel fillet (approx 100g/4oz), roughly flaked. Alternatively
*   substitute the same weight of ham, chicken, nuts or cubed, cooked*
*   root vegetables for the mackerel*
50g/2oz fresh spinach, roughly chopped
1 tsp each fresh chopped thyme and oregano, or 1/2 tsp each dried
salt and pepper

1. Heat the oil and briskly fry the mushrooms for 3 minutes.
2. Beat the tofu in a bowl with a wooden spoon till it is smooth, then add the soya milk, or soya milk and white wine mixed, and stir till you have a reasonably smooth cream.
3. Add the flaked mackerel (or other filling), spinach and herbs and season generously.
4. Pour the mixture into the pastry case and bake for 20 minutes in a moderately hot oven - 180C/350F/Gas Mark 4 . The flan will set but not rise as it would with eggs, nor go brown. However, the mixture of the white tofu, green spinach and ochre coloured mackerel is very pretty.

MAIN DISHES

MUSHROOM AND SUNFLOWER SEED FLAN
Serves 4
Dairy free; egg free; medium fat; 524 Kcal/portion

150g/6oz wholemeal flour
75g/3oz dairy free margarine
3 tbsp olive, peanut, walnut or other well flavoured oil
150g /6oz baby sweetcorns, cut in two or three pieces depending on size
2 heaped tbsp sunflower seeds
225g/8oz mushrooms, whole,, halved or quartered
75g/3oz fresh spinach, chopped fairly small
salt and pepper

1. Make the pastry by rubbing the margarine into the flour then adding enough water to make a firm dough. Roll it out and line a 20-22cm/8-9inch flan dish. Prick the bottom, line it with foil, weight it with beans or rice and bake it in a moderately hot oven - 180C/350F/Gas Mark 4. It should need about 15 minutes with the foil in, then 10 minutes without it to get nice and crisp.
2. Meanwhile, heat the oil in a heavy pan and add the corn and sunflower seeds. Fry briskly till they are lightly tanned all over.
3. Add the mushrooms, reduce the heat slightly and continue to cook for a couple of minutes. Then add the chopped spinach, stir well, cover the pan and cook for a further couple of minutes.
4. Remove the lid, season well, make sure the ingredients are well amalgamated then spoon them into the flan case.
5. Serve at once, warm or leave to cool and serve.

QUINOA AND CASHEW RISOTTO

Quinoa is a grain product grown in the Andes which tastes like a cross between barley and rice. It is delicious and entirely gluten free.

Serves 4

Dairy free; gluten free; egg free; low fat; 316 Kcal/portion

1 tbsp   olive oil
1 leek, finely sliced
1 stick celery, finely sliced
4 tbsp quinoa
300ml/1/2 pt water or wine and water mixed
200g/7oz tin water chestnuts
100g/4oz cashew nuts
2 tbsp sunflower seeds
juice of 1 lemon
salt and pepper
1 handful of fresh mint, chopped small

1. Heat the oil and cook the celery and leek till just soft.
2. Add the quinoa and the liquid, bring to the boil and cook gently for 15 minutes till the quinoa is soft and has absorbed the liquid - add more if necessary.
3. Drain the water chestnuts and halve them, then add to the mixture.
4. Brown the nuts and sunflower seeds in a dry pan then add them to the risotto along with lemon juice, salt and pepper to taste.
5. Just before serving stir in the fresh chopped mint. Serve warm or cold.

PEPPER, NUT AND TOFU SALAD

Serves 4
Dairy free; gluten free; egg free; medium fat; 338 Kcal/portion
4 tbsp olive oil
3 large green peppers, seeded and sliced
2 handfuls of cashews, hazelnuts or peanuts
1 heaped tsp coriander seeds
225g/8oz smoked tofu, diced
gluten free soya sauce
1. Heat the oil in a pan and gently cook the pepper till slightly softened.
2. Add the nuts and coriander seeds and continue to cook for a further five minutes or till the nuts are lightly browned.
3. Add the tofu and cook for a further couple of minutes to warm and slightly brown the tofu.
4. Season with soy sauce and serve at once.

PASTA WITH TOMATO SAUCE

Serves 4
Dairy free; gluten free; egg free; low fat; 336 Kcal/portion
450g/1lb rice noodles OR normal pasta if you can tolerate gluten & eggs
3 tbsp olive, soya, sunflower or rapeseed oil
2 medium onions, chopped fine
4 sticks celery, very finely chopped
100g/4oz mushrooms, sliced thinly
1 x 400g/14oz tin chopped tomatoes
150ml/5fl oz dry white wine or vegetable stock
2 tsp dried marjoram
salt and pepper
50g/2oz chopped ham, tongue or prawns (optional)
1. Heat the oil in a heavy pan and gently cook the onion and celery till soft; add the mushrooms and continue to cook for a few minutes.
2. Add the tomatoes, liquid, dried marjoram and a little seasoning.
3. Bring to the boil and simmer gently for 20 - 30 minutes.
4. Adjust the seasoning to taste and add the ham etc if using them.
5. Cook the rice noodles or pasta in plenty of fast boiling water till they are just cooked or *al dente.*
6. Drain the noodles quickly and turn them into a dish, spoon over the sauce and serve at once.

PASTA PRIMAVERA

Serves 4

Dairy free; gluten free; egg free; low fat; 581 Kcal/portion

450g/1lb rice noodles OR normal pasta if you can tolerate gluten & eggs
3 tbsp olive, soya, sunflower or rapeseed oil
2 leeks, sliced very thinly
4 sticks celery, very finely chopped
100g/4oz mushrooms, sliced thinly
1 x 200g/7 oz tin artichoke hearts, quartered
50g/2oz chopped ham, tongue or prawns (optional)
300ml/10fl oz soya cream or puréed silken tofu
150ml/5fl oz dry white wine or vegetable stock
juice 1/2 - 1 lemon
salt and pepper
a handful of parsley, finely chopped

1. Heat the oil in a heavy pan and gently cook the leek and celery till soft; add the mushrooms and continue to cook for a few minutes.

2. Add the artichoke hearts and the ham etc if you are using it.

3. Add the soya cream or tofu and the wine or stock. Mix well and allow to simmer for a few minutes.

4. Add the lemon juice and season to taste.

5. Cook the rice noodles or pasta in plenty of fast boiling water till they are just cooked or *al dente.* Drain the noodles quickly and turn them into a dish.

6. Stir the parsley into the sauce, spoon it over the noodles and serve.

SPINACH SOUFFLE

Serves 4

Dairy free; gluten free; low fat; 262 Kcal/portion

4 tbsp olive oil
2 leeks, trimmed and sliced very finely
100g/4oz mushrooms, sliced finely
450g/1lb young spinach leaves, washed, well dried & chopped small
200g/7oz silken tofu, puréed
salt and pepper
5 large egg yolks and 6 whites
1 tbsp sesame seeds

1. Heat the oil in a heavy pan and gently cook the leeks and mushrooms till they are quite soft.
2. Add the spinach, cover and cook till the spinach is almost puréed.
3. Add the tofu and season well.
4. Remove from the heat and stir in the egg yolks.
5. Whisk the egg whites till they just hold their shape in soft peaks. Stir 1/3 of the whites into the spinach mixture and fold in the rest.
6. Pour into a soufflé dish, sprinkle over the sesame seeds, and cook in a moderate hot oven (180C/350F/Gas Mark 4) for 20-25 minutes or till it is risen and golden. Serve at once.

COLD CHICKEN OR BEAN SALAD WITH APPLE

To turn this into a vegetarian dish substitute 450g/1lb cooked white haricot beans for the chicken.

Serves 4

Dairy free; gluten free; egg free; low fat; 323 Kcal/portion

1 small cooked chicken, the meat cut up small
the rind and juice of 2 lemons
1 tart eating apple, diced
1 small onion, chopped very fine
2 handfuls of parsley, roughly chopped
* salt and freshly ground black pepper*
2 - 3 tbsp olive oil

1. In a bowl mix the chicken, lemon rind, apple, onion and parsley.
2. Sprinkle with salt and freshly ground black pepper then add the lemon juice and olive oil. Mix it well together and serve.

CHICKEN & LEEK CRUMBLE/PIE

Serves 4

Dairy free; wheat free; egg free. With potato topping - low fat; 407 Kcal/portion; with crumble topping - medium fat; 624 Kcal/portion

1 chicken
4 medium leeks
900ml/11/2pt water or water
*   & white wine mixed*
small handful peppercorns
2 tsp dried marjoram
3 tbsp arrowroot
150ml/5fl oz cow's OR soya milk
salt

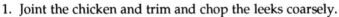

1. Joint the chicken and trim and chop the leeks coarsely.
2. Put both in a heavy pan with the water or wine and water mixed, the peppercorns and the marjoram.
3. Bring to the boil and simmer for 25 minutes or till the chicken is cooked. Remove the chicken from the pan and the meat from the bones.
4. Mix the arrowroot with the cow's/soya milk and add it to the cooking liquid. Mix well and continue to simmer till the liquid thickens. Season to taste with the salt.
5. Put the chicken pieces into a dish and pour over the leeks and juices.

POTATO TOPPING

Dairy free; gluten free; egg free
1 kilo/2lbs potatoes, scrubbed or peeled and cut up
a little soya milk, dairy free margarine, salt & pepper

1. Steam, boil or microwave the potatoes.
2. Mash them adding soya milk, margarine, salt and pepper to taste.
3. Cover the chicken with the potato and cook for 20 minutes in a moderate oven (5 minutes in a microwave) to reheat.

CRUMBLE TOPPING

dairy free; wheat free; egg free
225g/8oz oats, rolled or porridge
75g/3oz nuts, hazel, cashews or almonds, finely chopped
50g/2oz dairy free margarine and a pinch salt

1. If you want a fine crumble, process the oats for a couple of minutes.
2. Mix with the nuts and salt and rub in the margarine.
3. Spread over the chicken mixture and cook in a moderate oven (180C/350F/Gas Mark 4) for 30 minutes or till lightly tanned.

CHICKEN WITH OKRA
Serves 4
Dairy free; gluten free; egg free; low fat; 460 Kcal/portion
6 tbsp olive, soya, sunflower or rapeseed oil
4 joints of chicken or a whole small chicken, jointed
225g/8oz okra, topped and tailed and chopped roughly
225g/8oz baby sweet corns, halved
225g/8oz courgettes, sliced thickly
1 x 400g/14oz tin tomatoes, whole or chopped
240ml/8fl oz rough red wine or vegetable stock
2 generous tsp dried or 3 tsp fresh marjoram
salt, pepper and the juice 1 large lemon
1. In the oil, briskly fry the chicken joints on all sides till they start to tan.
2. Add the okra, corns and courgettes and continue to fry till the vegetables have also taken on a little colour.
3. Add the tomatoes (chop them up if they are whole), the red wine or stock, marjoram and seasoning. Bring to the boil, cover and simmer gently for 30 minutes or till the chicken is quite cooked.
4. Add the lemon juice and adjust the seasoning to taste before serving.

BARBECUES
Barbecues are ideal for anyone with a food intolerance as you can control exactly what goes into them.
Dairy free; gluten free; egg free
Meat. *For preference, use organically grown meat. Cut it in largish cubes. Marinade it for a couple of hours to tenderise it and keep it moist.*
Fish - *use solid fish such as tuna, mackerel , shark and shell fish; soft, white fish disintegrates.*
Vegetables & fruits - *juicy vegetables (celery, peppers, tomatoes, mushrooms, courgettes), root vegetables and onions, if they have been parcooked, firm fresh fruits and plump dried fruits all barbecue well.*
For each person allow *225g/8oz of food altogether and accompany it with a potato microwaved for a few minutes, then baked on the barbecue.*
Marinades. *Oil (olive, sunflower, rape or soya) with lemon juice, salt and pepper makes a good simple marinade. To be more exotic, add garlic, tomato purée, fresh chopped ginger, any dried herb or spice, wine, a little vinegar or a couple of tbsp of dairy or soya yoghurt if you want the marinade creamy. Make enough to just submerge the meat.*
Cooking. If you like your meat well done, cook it first, then add the vegetables and fruit; if rare cook all together. Turn frequently to prevent burning and baste continually with the marinade or oil.

STIR FRIES

Stir fries are excellent for anyone with food intolerance as you need only include the foods that you are happy with.

dairy free; gluten free; egg free

Per person

Allow 225g/8oz vegetables per person and make it up of as many different vegetables as you choose. Many of the supermarkets now sell ready mixed packs of stir fry vegetables. Root vegetables are fine but must be cut very thin to allow quick cooking; juicy vegetables such as cucumber and beans shoots are particularly good

If you like it spicy 1tsp each finely chopped garlic, fresh ginger root or fresh turmeric root are excellent.

Allow 50g/2oz of some kind of protein to go with your vegetables - ham, tongue, smoked mackerel, prawns etc or, if you would prefer to have a vegetarian stir fry, nuts (cashews, peanuts, flaked almonds) or seeds (sunflower, pumpkin or sesame).

2 tbsp oil - rapeseed, groundnut or a special stir fry oil are best

soya sauce, salt and pepper

1. Cut your vegetables into very thin slices or matchsticks - obviously leaving vegetables such as beanshoots whole.
2. Heat your oil in your wok till nearly smoking. If you do not have a wok you can make a very successful stir fry in a frying pan.
3. Add garlic, turmeric & ginger root; cook for a few minutes stirring continually.
4. Add the harder vegetables, turn the heat down a bit and allow them to cook for 5 minutes or till just softening.
5. Add the softer vegetables, turn the heat up again and cook briskly for a couple of minutes, stirring continuously.
6. Add your nuts (you can brown these in an oven or on a dry pan for extra flavour), seeds, meat or fish and soya sauce and seasoning to taste.
7. Serve at once.

DAIRY AND EGG FREE MOUSSAKA

Serves 4

Dairy free; gluten free; egg free; medium fat; 495 Kcal/portion

6-8 tbsp olive, soya, sunflower or rapeseed oil
2 largish aubergines, sliced
350g/12oz cooked lamb, cubed or pulled into bite size pieces
6 tomatoes, sliced or 1 x 225g/8oz tin chopped tomatoes
salt and pepper
1 heaped tsp dried marjoram
25g/1oz sunflower seeds
15g/1/2oz sesame seeds
1 tbsp olive oil
juice 1/2 - 1 lemon
200g/7oz silken tofu

1. Fry the aubergine slices in the oil until they are well tanned on each side and lay half of them out in the bottom of an ovenproof casserole.
2. Lay the lamb over the aubergine and cover it with the sliced tomato. Sprinkle this generously with salt and pepper and the marjoram.
3. Cover with the remains of the aubergine.
4. Purée the seeds with the olive oil, lemon juice and tofu in a food processor then spoon the mixture over the aubergine.
5. Cook in a moderate oven (180C/350F/Gas Mark 4) for 20-30 minutes or till the top is well browned. Serve at once.

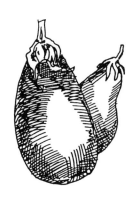

BRAISED LAMB WITH VEGETABLES

Serves 4
Dairy free; gluten free; egg free; low fat; 577 Kcal/portion

700-900g/1 1/2-2lb joint of lamb, a half leg or shoulder
4 cloves garlic, peeled but left whole
2 tbs olive, soya, sunflower or rapeseed oil
225g/8oz leeks, cleaned and sliced
225g/8oz sweet potatoes (or ordinary potatoes if you find sweet
*   potatoes too sweet) par-cooked then peeled, sliced thickly*
2 large or 4 small tomatoes, sliced
150g/6oz broccoli spears
plenty of salt and freshly ground black pepper
150ml/5fl oz dry white wine or vegetable stock

1. Cut four deep slits in the lamb and push the garlic cloves well in.
2. Pour the oil into the bottom of a deepish oven proof dish or casserole large enough to hold all the vegetables and the meat.
3. Lay the leeks out in the bottom of the casserole and cover them with the sliced potato. Season generously with salt and black pepper.
4. Lay the tomatoes on top of the potatoes then put the joint of lamb in the middle and arrange the broccoli spears around the outside.
5. Season again and pour the wine or stock over the top.
6. Cover the dish and cook it in a moderate oven (180C/350F/Gas Mark 4) for 40-55 minutes depending on whether you like your lamb pink or well cooked. Serve straight from the dish

POTATO & POLENTA BAKE WITH APPLE SAUCE

Serves 4

Gluten free; egg free; medium fat; 790 Kcal/portion
750g/11/2 bs floury old potatoes, scrubbed and diced, skins on
225g/8oz coarse polenta (fine will make it too mushy)
450ml/15fl oz milk
300ml/10fl oz water
salt and pepper
225g/8oz gorgonzola or dolcelatte cheese
1 tsp dried mixed herbs
25g/1oz butter or olive or good vegetable oil
750g/1 1/2 lbs cooking apples, peeled and chopped
5 cloves and1 tsp cinnamon
50g/2oz sugar
120ml/4fl oz water

1. Cook the potatoes on the hob or in a microwave until they are almost mushy, drain them and set them aside.
2. Cook the polenta in the milk and water for 15 - 20 minutes to absorb most of the liquid. Season generously then mix in the cheese and herbs.
3. Mix the polenta with the potatoes and pile it into a pie dish or fairly open casserole. Dot the top with butter or drip with oil and bake it in a medium oven (180C/250F/Gas Mark 4) for 30 minutes.
4. Meanwhile, cook the apples with the cloves, cinnamon, sugar and water. Remove the cloves and purée or sieve the apple.
5. Serve the bake with plenty of warm apple sauce.

HELPFUL HINTS WITH VEGETABLES

If you do not wish to serve your vegetables naked but don't want to use butter, dribble a little olive, nut, sunflower or even corn oil over them instead of adding a knob of butter. Olive oil is always delicious and full of mono-unsaturates; hazelnut or walnut oils taste more exotic although they are very expensive; sunflower is light in flavour and full of poly-unsaturates.

Roast potatoes need not be a thing of the past just because you do not want to use lard. Par-boil them as usual and roughen their outsides. Then roast in a couple of tbsp of olive, sunflower or corn oil.

CHRISTMAS DISHES

RICE 'BREAD' SAUCE - WITH SOYA MILK
Serves 8
Dairy free; gluten free; egg free; medium fat; 120 Kcal/portion

100 oz white pudding rice
900ml/1 1/2 pint fresh cow's milk OR 1 litre/1 3/4 pints soya milk
1-2 medium onion, stuck with 10-12 whole cloves
salt & 8-10 peppercorns
1 tsp sugar/fructose (optional)

1. Put the rice in a pan with the milk and the onion stuck with the cloves and the peppercorns.
2. Bring slowly to the boil and simmer very gently, taking care it does not stick or burn, for 20 - 30 minutes or till the rice is quite soft.
3. Remove the cloves from the onion and purée the milky rice in a food processor. Depending on how strong an onion flavour you like purée the onions with the mixture or remove them first.
4. Season to taste with salt and, if you are using the soya milk you may wish to add a little sugar as well.
5. Reheat gently in a pan or (better) in a microwave before serving.

QUINOA AND CASHEW STUFFING

Enough for 1 medium turkey
Dairy free; gluten free; egg free; high fat; 1093 Kcal. total
2 tbsp olive, sunflower or soya oil
1 medium onion, finely chopped
2 cloves garlic, crushed (optional)
1 large or 2 small sticks celery, chopped
100 g / 4 oz quinoa
1/2 tsp dried or 1 tsp fresh thyme
300ml/1/2pint water & 150ml/1/4 pint dry white wine
75g/3oz whole cashew nuts
a handful of parsley, chopped, salt, pepper & a dash of lemon juice
1. Heat the oil in a pan and gently cook the onion, garlic and celery till they are just soft.
2. Add the quinoa and the thyme, the water & the wine. Bring to the boil and simmer gently for 15-20 minutes adding a little more liquid if the mixture is drying up.
3. When the quinoa is soft add the nuts, parsley and salt, pepper and lemon juice to taste then use it to stuff the turkey.

GRAVY

Makes approx. 1 litre/1 3/4 pints gravy
Dairy free; gluten free; egg free; medium fat; 750 K/cal / litre
Giblets from the turkey with a carrot, onion, stick of celery, clove of garlic, mushroom stalk, tomato etc, roughly chopped plus a handful of peppercorns & a bayleaf
1.2litres/2pints water plus a dash of wine or sherry if available or 1.2litres/2pints Vecon stock
25g/1oz dairy free vegetable margarine or fat from the turkey
50g/2oz arrowroot
150ml/1/4 pint Marsala, port or red wine (optional)
salt & pepper
1. Put the giblets in a pan with the vegetables, herbs and water and bring to the boil. Simmer for 1 hour then strain.
2. Heat the turkey fat or vegetable margarine in a pan.
3. Mix the arrowroot with a little of the stock to make a thick paste then add to the fat in the pan. Heat gently, stirring continually, and gradually adding a little more stock, until mixture thickens.
5. Continue to cook for 15 minutes then add Marsala & season to taste.

CHICKPEA & CHESTNUT STUFFING

Enough for 1 medium turkey
Dairy free; gluten free; egg free; high fat; 923 Kcal. total
100g/4oz chestnut purée or whole tinned chestnuts
4 tbsp olive, sunflower, hazel or walnut oil
2 tbsp medium sweet sherry, marsala or port
100g/4oz tinned chick peas
2 tbsp sunflower seeds
salt and pepper
1. Purée the chestnuts or chestnut purée in a food processor with the oil and the sherry or wine till it is quite smooth and well amalgamated.
2. Add the chick peas and purée briefly if you want to keep some 'crunchiness' in the chick peas; if you want a totally smooth stuffing it does not matter how vigorously you purée them.
3. Remove from the processor. Add sunflower seeds & season to taste.
4. You can use the stuffing inside the bird, bake it in little balls alongside the bird - or use it as a paté on toast !

CHRISTMAS PUDDING ICE CREAM

This recipe was devised for Berrydales ices but you could use it with any other soya ice, or a cream based ice cream if you do not have a problem with dairy products but do with the gluten in Christmas pudding.
Serves 4 - 6 depending on appetite
Dairy free; gluten free; egg free; fat & calorie count dependant on ice cream
1 100ml tub each of Berrydales' Maple & walnut & Ginger & honey ices
25g/1oz each of raisins, currants, sultanas, mixed peel and glacé
        cherries (halved or quartered)
4 tbsp brandy
1. Soak the fruits for 30 minutes in 2 tbsp of the brandy.
2. Take the ices from the freezer and allow them to soften just enough to be able to mix them roughly together.
3. Mix the fruit into the ices and spoon the whole lot into a a pudding basin approximately 12 cm / 5 inches in diameter - press down firmly.
4. Refreeze the pudding and when you are ready to serve it, turn it out onto a plate like an ordinary Xmas pud.
5. Heat the remaining brandy in a metal soup ladle, light it with a match, pour it round the bottom of the pudding and serve immediately.

MIRIAM'S MINCE TART

Makes 2 x 350g / 12oz jars / 2 medium size tarts
Dairy free; gluten free; egg free; no added sugar; low fat; 555 Kcal./jar

1 or 2 flan cases made from wheat, oat or gluten free pastry - see p.36/7and
*   baked blind/or not, according to the paste*
100g /4oz each sultanas, raisins & currants, well washed
25g/1oz dried apricots, well washed
225g/8oz eating apples (2 apples), peeled
25g/1oz almonds
1-2tsp wheat free cinnamon
2 tsp wheat free mixed spice
if necessary, honey to taste, try 2 tsp)
juice of 1 orange & zest of 1 lemon, finely grated
2 tbsp brandy, if liked (it helps mincemeat to keep)

1. Mince finely the sultanas, raisins, apricots and half of the currants. Stir in the remaining currants, whole.
2. Mince the apples and almonds finely and stir them into the mixture.
3. Stir all the remaining ingredients into the minced mixture, adjusting the spices and honey to taste. (If you are not using brandy, you may want to add a little more orange juice to the mixture.)
4. Fill the flan cases with the mincemeat and use any left over pastry to make decorative lattice work or pastry balls to scatter over the top.
5. Bake for 20 minutes in a moderate oven (180F/350F/Gas Mark 4) or till the pastry is golden.
6. Pot any extra mixture into sterilised jars, and keep them chilled.

RITA GREER'S CHRISTMAS PUDDING
Serves 8
Dairy free; gluten free; egg free; fruit sugar only; low fat; 275 Kcal/portion

40g/11/2 oz fructose or 50g/2oz sugar
25g/1oz soya flour;
125g/5oz ground brown rice
25g/1oz split pea flour
1 pkt 'Easy bake' yeast
1/2 tsp <u>each</u> wheat free mixed spice,
     cinnamon & nutmeg
300ml/1/2 pint orange juice
50g/2oz soft dairy free margarine
1 small eating apple
1 small carrot
325g/11oz dried mixed fruit
grated rinds 1 lemon & 1 orange

1. Mix the sugar, soya flour, ground rice, split pea flour, yeast and spices well together.
2. Add the orange juice and the margarine and grate in the apple and carrot.
3. Beat until blended smooth then add the fruit & rinds and mix well.
4. Grease a 1 1/4 litre/2 1/2 pint pudding basin and spoon in the mixture. Tie on a double greaseproof lid and make a string handle.
8. Lower the basin into a large saucepan 1/3 full of water, cover tightly and steam for at least 1 1/2 hours. Decant as usual to serve.

NO-BUTTER BRANDY BUTTER
Makes enough for 8 good servings
Dairy free; gluten free; egg free; fruit sugar only; high fat; 170 Kcal/portion
100g/4oz dairy free margarine or spread
75g/3oz fructose OR 100g/4oz pale muscovado sugar
4 tbsp brandy
Beat the margarine hard with the sugar till it is light and fluffy. Add the brandy to taste.

ANNA'S RICH FRUIT CAKE

Serves 10

Dairy free; gluten free; no added sugar; low fat; 3600 Kcal/cake

50g/2oz dried apricots, washed & soaked
100g/4oz block of dates, chopped & all stones removed
150ml/1/4 pint water
75g/3oz soft dairy free margarine
3 eggs, beaten
125g/5oz rice flour plus 75g/3oz soya flour
2 tsp wheat free baking powder
1 1/2 tsp wheat free mixed spice
25g/1oz ground almonds or ground toasted hazelnuts
625g/1 lb 6oz mixed raisins, currants & sultanas, washed
zest 1/2 an orange, finely grated
1 tbsp brandy (optional) and a few drops of almond essence

1. Heat the oven to 160C/325F/Gas Mark 3. Grease an 18cm/7inch tin & line with greased greaseproof paper.
2. Cook the apricots and dates together in the water, simmering for about 15 minutes. Cool a little, then put the fruit and the cooking liquid into a blender and process till smooth.
3. Add the margarine and process again.
4. Transfer to a large bowl & beat in the eggs, a little at a time.
5. Sieve together the flours, baking powder and spice. Stir in the wet mixture, then the nuts, mixed fruit, orange zest, brandy or whisky and the almond essence. The mixture should be soft enough to drop from a spoon, but too thick to pour.
6. Spoon the mixture into the tin and hollow the top slightly.
7. Bake for 30 minutes, then reduce the heat to 150℃/300℉/Gas Mark 2 and bake for another hour, covering the top loosely with foil. Test with a skewer. Leave to cool for a minute in the tin before turning onto a rack .

WHITE CHRISTMAS ICING

Dairy free; gluten free; egg free; low fat; 2000 Kcal/cake
700 g / 1 1/2 lb icing sugar
approx. 12 tbsp lemon juice
1 dsp glycerine
In an electric mixer beat the icing sugar and the glycerine, gradually adding lemon juice till the mixture reaches spreading consistency.

DESSERTS

DAIRY FREE RICE PUDDING
Serves 4
Dairy free; gluten free; egg free; fruit sugar only; low fat; 179 Kcal/portion

100g/4oz Carolina pudding rice
600ml/1pt natural fruit juice. We used prune juice which needed no
extra sweetening and made a wonderful 'black' pudding but
there is no reason why you should not use apple, pear or
cranberry juice although the latter may need extra sweetening
1-2 tbsp fruit concentrate, if needed

1. Put the rice into a 1.2litre/2pint pudding dish.
2. Taste the juice and, remembering that it will get concentrated and therefore sweeter in the cooking, add a little extra fruit concentrate if you do not think it sweet enough.
3. Pour the juice into the rice and stir gently till it is well mixed.
4. Cook for 2 1/2 hours in a low oven (150 C / 300 F / Gas Mark 2), stirring once or twice during the cooking to make sure it doesn't stick.
5. Serve warm or cold, alone or with soya, goat or sheep yoghurt.

SUEDOISE OF PEACHES

Serves 6

Dairy free; gluten free; egg free; fruit sugar only; low fat; 59 Kcal/portion

*6 large ripe peaches plus 700g/1 1/2 lb other peaches - these do not need
    to be in such good condition*
300ml/10fl oz water
25g/1oz fructose OR 40g/1 1/2oxs raw cane sugar
juice 1 lemon

1. Peel and halve or quarter the large peaches carefully.
2. Put the water into a pan with the fructose or sugar. Bring it to the boil slowly to allow the fructose to melt and cook it for 2 minutes.
3. Lower in the peaches and simmer them for no more than 5 minutes.
4. Lift them out with a perforated spoon, put them in a deep dish and pour half the syrup over them.
5. Peel and chop the remaining peaches and add them to the remaining syrup with the lemon juice.
6. Bring the peaches back to the boil and simmer them gently for 45 minutes, making sure that they do not burn, until you have reduced them to a 'marmalade'.
7. Lift the large peaches out of the syrup and reduce this by boiling briskly for about 10 minutes - take care that it does not caramelise.
8. Spoon the 'marmalade' into a serving dish, arrange the halved or quartered peaches on top and pour over the reduced syrup.
9. Serve alone or with cream, soya cream, yoghurt or ice cream.

APPLE SOUFFLE

Serves 4-6

Dairy free; gluten free; fruit sugar only; low fat; 125 Kcal/portion
450g/1lb Bramley apples, peeled and cored
2 tbsp fructose, fruit concentrate OR muscovado sugar
1 tbsp gluten free cornflour
75ml/2 1/2fl oz Calvados or other suitable liqueur
3 whole eggs plus 1 white

1. Cook the apples with the sweetener and a couple of tbsp of water for 10 - 15 minutes or till they are totally soft.
2. Mix the cornflour with a little apple purée then return to the heat and cook gently for a couple of minutes till it thickens slightly. Add the liqueur.
3. Separate the eggs and stir the yolks into the apple.
4. Whisk the white till they form soft peaks. Stir in 1/3 of the white into the mixture then fold in the rest.
5. Spoon the mixture into a soufflé dish or individual ramekin dishes and bake in a pre-heated oven (190C/375F/Gas Mark 5) for 15-20 minutes for the big dish or 10-15 minutes for the individuals - or till they are slightly risen and the tops lightly tanned. Serve at once.

GLUTEN AND DAIRY FREE APPLE FLAN

Serves 4

Dairy free; gluten free; egg free; no added sugar; medium fat; 525 Kcal/portion
One 20-23cm/8-9 inch wheat, oat or gluten free flan case - see p 36/7- baked blind
3 large Bramley cooking apples
6 tbsp silken tofu
1 heaped tsp gluten free cornflour
juice of 2 large oranges and 1 large lemon

1. Liquidise the tofu with the cornflour and the juices.
2. Peel and chop the apples roughly and pile them in the cooked case.
3. Pour the tofu mixture over the top (if it is not thin enough to pour 'thickly', add a little more orange juice).
4. Bake for 20 minutes in a cool oven (170C/325F/Gas Mark 3) - the apples should be just cooked but still slightly crunchy and the top of the pie lightly browned.
5. Serve warm or cold.

UPSIDE DOWN TOFU CHEESECAKE
Serves 4
Dairy free; gluten free; egg free; fruit sugar only; medium fat; 395 Kcal/portion

400g/14oz silken tofu
75g/3oz fructose OR 100g/4oz raw cane sugar
1 level tsp agar agar
150ml/5fl oz mixed fresh orange and lemon juice, in whatever proportion
       you fancy
50g/2oz ground almonds
50g/2oz plump prunes chopped fine, or sultanas
75g/3oz finely crumbed biscuit, dairy or gluten free if required
25g/1oz dairy free margarine

1. Purée the tofu in a processor with the fructose or sugar.
2. Mix the agar agar in a small bowl with the fruit juice and heat it gently in the microwave or over hot water till the agar agar has melted.
3. Mix it into the tofu along with the almonds and prunes or sultanas.
4. Spoon the mixture into a suitable size flan dish or bowl.
5. Mix the crushed biscuits with the melted margarine or butter and spooon it over the top of the cheesecake.
6. Chill well before serving.

SOYA 'MILK' SHAKE
Per person
Dairy free; gluten free; egg free; fruit sugar only; low fat; 68 Kcal/portion
100g/4oz fresh fruit-strawberry, banana etc
4 tbsp plain or fruit soya yoghurt
1 tbsp fruit concentrate
4 tbsp vanilla or fruit soya ice cream
1. Purée the fruit, yoghurt and concentrate thoroughly in a liquidiser.
2. Add the ice cream and purée again.
3. Check the flavour and add more concentrate if necessary.
4. Serve at once.

SOYA FRUIT FOOL

Serves 4.

Dairy free; gluten free; egg free; fruit sugar only; low fat; 157 Kcal/portion
100g/4oz fresh strawberries or any other fruit you fancy
100ml/3fl oz fruit concentrate
juice 1/2 - 1 lemon
1 tsp agar agar
400g /13fl oz plain soya yoghurt

1. Purée the fruits in a processor, keeping out a couple for decoration.
2. Mix the concentrate with the agar agar and heat gently in a microwave or over hot water till melted.
3. In a bowl, beat the yoghurt with a spoon till it is smooth, then add the fruit purée and concentrate.
4. Add the lemon juice to taste and more fruit concentrate if needed.
5. Pour into glasses, decorate with the fruit and chill.

RED FRUIT SALAD

Feel free to use any other combinations of red fruits that you fancy
Serves 4

Dairy free; gluten free; egg free; no added sugar; low fat; 64 Kcal/portion
225g/8oz stoned cherries, preferably dark ones
225g/8oz firm red plums, stoned and sliced
225g/8oz fresh raspberries or strawberries -
*   if the latter they should be hulled*
*   and   halved*
2 lemons
2 oranges

1. Divide the fruit between the four dishes.
2. Squeeze the oranges and lemons, mix their juices and pour them over the fruits.
3. Serve the salad well chilled. You can serve soya cream or yoghurt with it if you like, but I think it detracts from the deliciously fresh flavour imparted by the juices.
NB. If the fruits are very tart you may need a little sweetening. If so, use a tbsp of fruit concentrate mixed in with the fruit juices.

SUMMER FRUIT AND NUT CRUMBLE

Serves 4

Dairy free; gluten free; egg free; fruit sugar only; low fat; 193 Kcal/portion

1kilo/2lb mixed soft summer fruits - raspberries, loganberries,
      strawberries, currants, bilberries etc
fructose or apple or pear concentrate to taste
75g/3oz toasted hazelnuts and 75g/3oz toasted flaked almonds **OR** *75g/3oz either nut mixed with 75g/3oz wholemeal flour*

1. Put the fruits in a pan or a microwave dish with about 20cm/1inch water in the bottom and cook gently for 10-15 minutes (4-6 minutes in a microwave on high) or till the fruits are soft without being mushy.
2. Sweeten to taste with the fructose or fruit concentrate - if the fruits are sweet you may not need any extra sweetening at all. Drain off the excess juice and save it to serve with the pudding.
3. Chop the nuts in a processor or liquidiser until they are as fine as rough breadcrumbs. If you are using them, mix the nuts with the breadcrumbs.
4. Spoon the fruit into an ovenproof dish & cover with the crumble mixture.
5. Bake in a moderate oven (180C/350F/Gas Mark 4) for 20-30 minutes or till the top is slightly crunchy and browned.
6. Serve with soya cream or yoghurt and the warmed fruit juices.

HOT FRUIT COMPOTE

Serves 4-6

Dairy free; gluten free; egg free; fruit sugar only; low fat; 51 Kcal/portion

450g/1lb mixed dried fruits - apricots, apples, prunes, large raisins, figs etc
450ml/3/4 pint water or 1/2 pint water and 1/4 pint red wine
1-2 tbsp fruit concentrate, fructose, honey or raw cane sugar - if needed
thinly pared rind of a small lemon or 2 tbsp lemon juice
stick of cinnamon or 1 level tsp ground cinnamon

1. Unless the fruit is very plump, soak it overnight, then drain it and discard the water.
2. Heat the fresh water, or wine and water, sweetener, lemon rind or juice and cinnamon gently in a pan. Add the fruit and simmer for 15 minutes or till it is cooked.
3. Remove the fruit into a bowl and continue to simmer the juice gently for a further 20 minutes till it is thickened and slightly reduced.
4. Pour the juice over the fruit and serve the compote warm or cold, plain or with cream, yoghurt, soya cream or ice cream.

29

DAIRY FREE CHOCOLATE PROFITEROLES
Serves 6
Dairy free ; medium fat; 549 Kcal/portion

Profiteroles:	*220ml/8fl oz water*
	75g/3oz dairy free margarine
	100g/4 oz plain white flour
	3 medium eggs
Filling:	*25g/1oz cocoa powder*
	15g/1/2oz cornflour
	300ml/10fl oz soya milk
	50g/2oz raw cane sugar
	75g/3oz good quality plain chocolate
	1 tbsp brandy or water
	225g/8oz puréed silken tofu
Sauce:	*225g/8oz good quality plain chocolate*
	12-14 tbsp water
	2 tbsp brandy (optional)

1. Heat the water & margarine till boiling. Sift the flour and tip it all at once itno the liquid. Beat thoroughly till the mixture is smooth and comes away from the sides of the pan.
2. Add the eggs gradually, beating all the time, until the dough is smooth and shiny.
3. Spoon walnut sized dollops of the dough onto some foil or greaseproof paper and bake in a preheated, hot oven (220C/425F/Gas Mark 7) for 15 - 20 minutes - the profiteroles should be tanned and firm to the touch.
4. Remove them from the oven and, as soon as possible, split them and remove any uncooked dough from the inside; leave them to cool.
5. Mix the cocoa and cornflour in a pan. Gradually add the milk, heating and stirring gently, until you have a smooth sauce.
6. Add the sugar and chocolate, broken up and continue to cook till both are melted. Add the brandy if you want to use it, if not, a little water and allow the sauce to cool.
7. When almost cold, mix in the tofu and stir thoroughly. Fill the profiteroles with this mixture when you are nearly ready to use them.
8. For the sauce, melt the chocolate with the water over a very gentle heat. When quite smooth, add the brandy.
9. Thin with a little more water if it is too thick then pour over the filled profiteroles just before serving.

GOOEY CHOCCY MOUSSE

Serves 4

Dairy free; gluten free; high fat; 336 Kcal/portion

150g/6oz dairy & gluten
free black chocolate
3 eggs
4 tbsp creamed tofu
2 tbspn brandy
40g/1 1/2oz finely chopped stem ginger
25g/1oz chopped pistachio nuts

1. Melt the chocolate over hot water or in a microwave.
2. Purée the tofu with the egg yolks and stir them thoroughly into the chocolate - you may need to keep the bowl over hot water to prevent the chocolate cooling and becoming unmanageable.
3. Add the brandy, stem ginger and pistachio nuts (reserving a few to sprinkle over the top) and mix thoroughly.
4. Whisk the egg whites till they hold their shape in soft peaks. Stir 1/3 of the egg whites into the chocolate mixture to lighten it, then fold in the remainder making sure that it is really well amalgamated.
5. Pour into four glasses or ramekin dishes, sprinkle over the remaining chopped pistachios. Chill till ready to serve.

FRUIT AND NUT CAROB 'CHOCOLATES'

Makes approx. 15

Dairy free; gluten free; egg free; no added sugar; low fat; 70 Kcal/each

Delicious after dinner bonbons or treats for children who are not allowed 'ordinary' sweets. If necessary you can substitute extra fruit for the nuts.

25g/1oz pre-softened prunes or dried apricots
250g/1oz sultanas or raisins
25g/1oz dried apple, or fig, or date
25g/1oz flaked almonds, hazelnuts, walnuts or any combination thereof
60g/2 1/2oz plain carob bar
juice of 1/2 a lemon

1. Chop the fruits and nuts in a food processor till fairly small.
2. Melt the carob bar in a microwave (1 minute on high) or over hot water. Mix it thoroughly into the fruit & nuts; add lemon juice to taste.
4. Roll the chocolates into small balls and chill before serving.

BAKING

EGGLESS FRUIT CAKE
Serves 8 - 10
Dairy free; egg free; medium fat; 3966 Kcal/cake

225g/8oz dairy free vegetable margarine
150/6oz raw cane muscovado sugar **OR** *100g/4oz fructose*
rind and juice of 2 oranges and 1/2 lemon
225g/8oz self raising flour, wholemeal or white or half and half (all
*   wholemeal will give a rather 'bready' texture to the cake)*
3 level tsp baking powder
4 tbsp tofu, creamed in a food processor
50g/2oz ground almonds
50g/2oz flaked almonds
100g/4oz each sultanas and raisins

1. Cream the margarine and sugar together until light and fluffy.
2. Beat in the fruit rind and juice, then the tofu along with 4 tbsp of the flour mixed with the baking powder.
3. Carefully fold in the rest of the flour along with the ground and flaked almonds and the dried fruit. If the mixture is too dry, add a little more orange juice.
4. Grease and 18cm/7inch tin and spoon in the mixture mounding it slightly in the middle as without eggs the mixture will sink slightly as it cooks rather than rising. Bake the cake in a moderately cool oven (150C/300F/Gas Mark 2) for 1 1/2 hours.
5. Remove from the oven, cool slightly then decant onto a rack.

SUGAR FREE OAT BASED FLAPJACKS

These are delicious, if rather crumbly, flapjacks. If your children do not like the nuts or seeds replace them with an extra 50g of oats.
Makes 8 - 10 flapjacks
Dairy free; wheat free; egg free; fruit sugar only; medium fat; 250 Kcal/flapjack

100g/4oz   dairy free margarine
20ml/4fl oz apple or apple and pear concentrate
225g/8oz jumbo or porridge oats
50g/2oz pine kernels or sunflower seeds

1. Melt the margarine with the fruit concentrate.
2. Lightly process the oats in a food processor or liquidiser; this will help them to stick together better.
3. Stir the oats, nuts and/or seeds into the margarine and concentrate and mix them well together.
4. With your fingers or a spatula press the mixture out in a thinnish layer in the botton of a metal or pyrex flan dish.
5. Cook the biscuits for 20 minutes in a cool oven (150C/350F/Gas Mark 3) or till they are lightly tanned.
6. As soon as they are cooked, section them with a knife and allow them to cool.
7. Remove carefully from the tin as they are very crumbly and store in a box or in the freezer.

LEMON SHORTBREAD
Makes 10-15 soft but tasty biscuits
*Dairy free; gluten free; egg free; fruit sugar
only; high fat; 155 Kcal / biscuit*
100g/4oz dairy free margarine
75g/3oz fructose OR 100g/4oz raw cane sugar
grated rind of 1/2 lemon
1 tbsp lemon juice
50g/2oz brown rice flour
100g/4oz ground almonds

1. Beat the margarine with the fructose or sugar, lemon rind and juice.
2. Beat in the rice flour and ground almonds.
3. Spoon into a baking tray and flatten out to finger thickness.
4. Bake in a very low oven (125C/275F/Gas Mark 2) for 45 minutes to 1 hour or till the biscuits are lightly tanned.
5. Cut carefully into biscuit shapes with a sharp knife, allow to cool slightly, then remove carefully onto a wire rack with a spatula and allow to cool completely.

LEMON OR ORANGE CAKE
Dairy free; egg free; fruit sugar only; low fat; 1703 Kcal/cake
100g/4oz dairy free margarine
100g/4oz raw cane muscovado sugar OR 75g/3oz fructose
2 level tsp baking powder
150g/6oz self raising flour, wholemeal, white or a mixture of the two
rind and juice of 2 lemons or 2 small oranges
120ml/4fl oz silken tofu, puréed in a food processor

1. Cream together the margarine and sugar or fructose till light.
2. Beat in the lemon rind, the juice and the tofu.
3. Fold in the flour and baking powder.
4. Spoon the mixture into a greased and lined round or oblong baking tin and bake for 40 minutes at 160C/325F/Gas Mark 3 1/2.
5. Remove from the tin and cool on a rack before eating .

CHOCOLATE FUDGE BROWNIE CAKE

Dairy free; gluten free; egg free; fruit sugar only; medium fat; 2483 Kcal/cake

75g/3oz dairy free margarine
250g/9oz raw cane muscovado sugar OR 175g/6oz fructose
3 level tbsp gluten free cocoa powder
100ml/3 1/2fl oz boiling water
100g/4oz silken tofu, puréed in a food processor
125g/5oz soya flour and 50g/2oz brown rice flour
3 heaped tsp gluten free baking powder

1. Beat the margarine with the sugar or fructose till light and fluffy.
2. Melt the cocoa in the boiling water and beat it into the margarine mixture along with the tofu.
3. Thoroughly fold in the flour mixed with the baking powder.
4. Spoon into a non-stick or loose-bottomed cake tin and bake for 30 minutes in a moderate oven - 170C/325F/Gas Mark 3.
5. Turn onto a rack and cool before eating.

DAIRY FREE, OAT BASED GINGERBREAD

Dairy free; wheat free; medium fat; 3271 Kcal/loaf

100g/4oz dairy free margarine
100g/4oz raw cane demerara or dark muscovado sugar
350g/12oz black treacle
4 eggs
225g/8oz rolled/porridge oats, powdered in a processor
1 heaped tsp baking powder
2 tsp ground ginger
1 heaped tsp each mixed spice and ground cinnamon

1. Melt the margarine, sugar and treacle together in a pan or microwave. Draw off the heat.
2. Beat the eggs into the melted mixture followed by the oats, baking powder and spices.
3. Pour into a greased loaf tin or cake tin and bake in a moderately cool oven (325F/160C/Gas Mark 3) for 45 minutes or till a skewer comes out clean.
4. Take out of the oven and the tin and cool on a rack.

OAT BASED PASTRY
The oats make a delicious but very crumbly pastry.
Serves 8
Dairy free; wheat free; egg free; no added sugar; high fat; 1814 Kcal / flan

225g/8oz jumbo or porridge oats, powdered in a food processor
125g/5oz dairy free vegetable margarine OR butter

1. Rub the fat into the oats as you would for shortcrust pastry, getting the two as well amalgamated as possible.
2. With your hands press the paste over the bottom and up the sides of a 200cm/8 inch flan dish, reserving scraps for decoration.
3. To bake blind, bake for 20 minutes in a 160C/325F/Gas Mark 3 or till the paste is tanned.

OAT BREAD
Makes 2 x 450g/1lb loaves
Dairy free; wheat free; egg free; medium fat; 885 Kcal/loaf

25g/1oz fresh yeast or 1 x 7g sachet fast acting dried yeast
400ml/14fl oz warm water
1 1/2 tsp salt
1 tbsp raw cane sugar OR 1 dspfructose
1 tbsp vegetable oil
400g/1lb12oz rolled oats, puréed in a food processor

1. Place flour and salt in a mixing bowl or food processor.
2. Dissolve the fresh yeast in the warm water, add the salt, sugar and oil, and finally the oat flour. If using dried yeast, mix the yeast, salt and sugar into the flour, then add the water and oil.
3. Mix well together then beat hard by hand or in a mixer or processor for at least 5 minutes - if you don't the loaf will not rise at all.
4. Spoon the mixture into one or two well greased loaf tins and bake in a moderate oven (180C/350F/Gas mark 4) for 1 hour.
5. Cool on a wire rack and leave to get completely cold before cutting.

RITA GREER'S GLUTEN FREE BROWN LOAF

Dairy free; gluten free; egg free; medium fat; 856 Kcal/loaf
1 pkt 'Easy Bake' yeast
1 heaped tsp raw cane sugar **OR** 1 level tsp fructose
25g/1oz soya flour

115g/4 1/2oz ground brown rice
20g/3/4oz yellow split pea flour
2 tsp dried pectin to bind
15g/1/2oz ground almonds
3 pinches salt
3 tsp vegetable oil
1 heaped tsp carob powder
250ml/9fl oz warm water

1. Preheat oven to 180C/350F/Gas Mark 4.
2. Put all the ingredients except the water into a bowl and mix well with the hands, breaking up any lumps.
3. Stir in the water.
4. Mix, then beat, with a wooden spoon. (Do not use an electric beater as this will make the batter too tough.)
5. Grease a medium size loaf tin with oil and dust with maize or potato flour, then use a wooden spoon to place the mixture in the tin.
6. Bake for 1 hour till well risen, golden and crusty. Turn out onto a wire rack to cool and do not cut till cold.

GLUTEN FREE PASTRY

Serves 6
Dairy free; gluten free; egg free; high fat; 1459 Kcal/flan
100g/4oz brown rice flour
100g/4oz soya flour
1/2 tsp gluten free baking powder
100g/4oz dairy free margarine
2 tbsp water **OR** 1 egg
1. Mix the flours with the baking powder.
2. Mix in the margarine by hand and moisten with a little water or an egg, if you can tolerate them.
3. Press into the bottom and up the sides of a 20-23cm/8-9 inch flan dish.
4. Bake blind (20 minutes in a moderate oven - 180C/350F/Gas Mark 4) or not as required.

PRODUCT INFORMATION

Where the manufacturer is well represented in health food shops we have only given the brand name; where the product is less easily available we have given a contact telephone number.

However, not all products sold under a particular brand name will be dairy, gluten, egg or sugar free so CHECK THE INGREDIENTS LABEL ON EVERY PRODUCT BEFORE BUYING.

GENERAL

Green Farm Foodwatch of Burwash Common, East Sussex TN19 7LX Tel. 0435 882482 and Optional Health of Pond Approach, Homer Green, High Wycombe, Bucks HP15 6HR Tel. 0494 712 333 do a wide range of mail order alternative foods. Call them for their catalogues.

CHOLESTEROL FREE St Giles Lite Egg

COFFEE & TEA

Coffee substitutes	Bambu, Caro, Symingtons dandelion
Decaffeinated coffee	Simon Levelt
Decaffeinated tea	Luaka, St James', Twinings

EGG FREE

Mayonnaise/sauce	Direct Foods Mountain Spring Mayonnaise, Meridian Mayo, St Giles/Life
Replacers	Ener-G, Rite Diet
Sandwich spread	St Giles/Duchesse , Green Cuisine

DAIRY FREE

Cheese/Cheese spread	Fromsoya, Green Dragon Scheese, Marigold, Redwood
Confectionary	Carob Confectionary, Dove Cottage. Plamil
'Ice Cream'	Berrydales, Dayvilles, Elysia, Genice, Granose, Ice Dream, Marinelli(fruit sugar only), So-Good
Margarines & spreads	DP Pure, Golden Rose, Granose, Outline, Sainsburys Dairy Free, Suma, Tomor, Vitaquell
Pastry mix	Diet care (0273 417157)
Soya cream	Granose
Soya desserts	Granose Sweet Sensation, Granovita, Provamel, Sogood, Sojasun, Unisoy
Soya drinks	Alpro, Soya Health Foods
Soya milks	Bonsoy, Granose, Granovita, Plamil, Provamel, So-Good, Sojal, Sunrise, Unisoy
Soya yoghurt	Granose, So-good
Sweets	Carob Confectionary, Exquisite Confections
Tofu	Cauldron, Granose Organic, Paul's, Mori-nu

GOAT/SHEEP PRODUCTS

Cheese	Shepherd's Purse, Sussex Weald
Dried milk powder	Sussex Weald. Tregaron
Infant formula	Nanny
Milk	Sussex Weald, Sutton dairy
Yoghurt	Woodlands Park

REDUCED SUGAR / NO ADDED SUGAR

Biscuits	Prewetts
Cakes	Rite Diet diabetic
Fructose	Dietade Fruit sugar, Fruisana
Fruit concentrates	Meridian
Jams/spreads	Meridian, Plamil, Sunwheel, Thursday Cottage, Wh. Earth
Mincemeat	Meridian
Peanut butter	Whole Earth
Sauces	Whole Earth tomato ketchup
Sweets	Exquisite Confections, Grizzly bars, Holly Mill, JRJ Fruit leathers, Plamil, Prewetts fruit bars, Simpkins